A B C D E F
G H I J
K L M N O P
Q R S T
U V W X Y Z

G is for Garden, an Alphabet Book, by Jamie B. Banta. Copyright © 2018 by Jamie B. Banta
All rights reserved

This book or parts thereof may not be reproduced in any form, stored in a retrieval system, or transmitted in any form by any means, without prior written permission of the publisher, except as provided by United States of America copyright law.

Published in the United States of America by:
Chara Press, PO Box 79, Keasbey, New Jersey 08832

Cover design and Interior Design: Jamie B. Banta, JamieBeeDesigns.com
Photographs: Jamie B. Banta

Paperback ISBN: 978-1-944705-02-2
Hardcover ISBN: 978-1-944705-10-7

Printed in the United States of America

Publisher's Cataloging-In-Publication Data

Names:	Banta, Jamie B., author.
Title:	G is for garden : an alphabet book / Jamie B. Banta.
Description:	Keasbey, New Jersey : Chara Press, [2018]	Includes index.	Audience: Age Level: 3 - 8; Grade Level: P - 3.	Summary: Take a walk in a garden. What could you see? Let's look and discover, from A to Z! From Ants and Apples to Zinnia and BuzzZZ, young readers learning their ABCs can have fun discovering new words and some of the different plants, flowers, animals, and other surprises you can find in a garden. This book is fully illustrated with vivid photographs. An index at the end of the book shares more information about the pictures for adults and children to enjoy reading together.--Publisher.
Identifiers:	ISBN: 978-1-944705-02-2 (paperback)	978-1-944705-10-7 (hardcover)	LCCN: 2018902577
Subjects:	LCSH: Gardens--Juvenile literature.	Flowers--Juvenile literature.	Plants--Juvenile literature.	Garden animals--Juvenile literature.	Insects--Juvenile literature.	Alphabet books.	CYAC: Gardens.	Flowers.	Plants.	Garden animals.	Insects.	Alphabet.	BISAC: JUVENILE NONFICTION / Science & Nature / Flowers & Plants.	JUVENILE NONFICTION / Readers / Beginner.	JUVENILE NONFICTION / Concepts / Alphabet.
Classification:	LCC: SB457 .B36 2018	DDC: 635.022/2--dc23

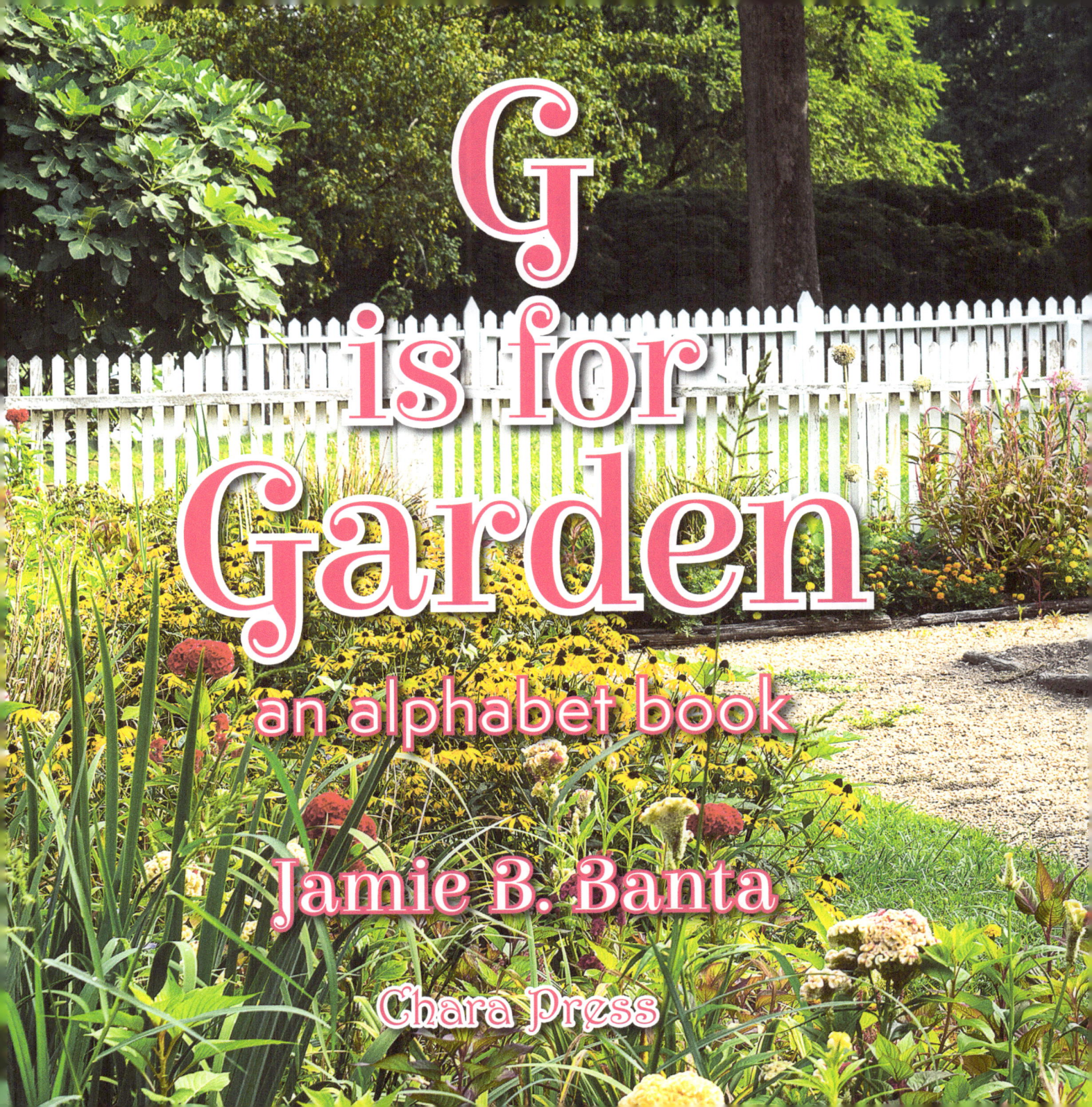

For
Mackenzie Lee Rose
who loves roses.
(Of course!)

Take a walk in a garden.
What could you see?
Let's look and discover,
from A to Z!

is for ants

and apples.

and bud.

and cactus.

D is for discover

and dandelion.

and flowers.

and green.

i is for itchy

and icy.

J

is for juicy

and jumbled.

K
is for keep

and leaf.

M
is for morning glory

and needles.

and orchid.

and quiet.

R

is for rose

and rabbit.

and sunflower.

and tulips.

and under.

and vine.

W
is for water

X

is for explore

and young.

About the Pictures

A   Ants love peony buds. They want to eat the sweet sap that leaks from the buds.
Apples are a sweet healthy food that grow on trees.

B   A little skipper butterfly loves to flit from flower to flower and sips on nectar.
A hibiscus flower starts as a small bud.

C   A colorful bird of paradise flower needs warm weather and a sunny spot to grow.
A cereus cactus blooms at night, but you can see the white flowers in early morning.

D   Did you discover the shiny green bee hunting for nectar in the passion flower?
Dandelions are such a cheerful yellow. I wish they weren't a weed.

E   It's nice to sit in the garden in the evening and watch the sunset.
Some daffodils are trying to come up early. They're not afraid of the snow.

F   Many gardens have fences to protect the plants.
Chrysanthemum flowers give us cheerful color in our gardens in the fall.

G   A garden can be big or small. You can grow flowers, bushes, trees, and even vegetables.
Flowers come in all colors of the rainbow — even green like these orchids!

H Holly is an evergreen bush with bright red berries.
A noisy cicada is hidden in a privet bush. This bug sings by making a very loud buzz.

I Watch out for poison ivy's itchy leaves of three! Leave them be.
Icy winter weather makes trees glitter.

J A juicy mango fruit ripens high in its very tall tree.
A jumble of leaves makes piles of color on the lawn in the fall.

K Sometimes you can pick and keep a flower. Remember to ask first and say please!
Little vines twine and twirl and make a curly knot.

L A lilac is favorite shrub to grow in gardens because of its sweet smell and lovely blooms.
A big papaya leaf spreads out like an umbrella and make shade for its fruit.

M The morning glory blooms in the morning. Each flower only lasts for a single day.
Little mushrooms may pop up in the garden. They are a fungi, not a plant.

N Tiny new fern fronds peep out of the ground.
A pine tree has needles instead of flat leaves. It stays green even in winter.

O This orange daylily blooms in summer. A daylily can also be yellow or red.
Orchids are a special plant. Some grow on tree branches and dangle their roots in the air.

P A big purple passionflower grows on a vine. It is tropical plant that needs lots of sun.
This bright pink bromeliad is a strange-looking tropical plant.

Q A squirrel is quick animal. It climbs trees and looks for seeds and fruit to eat.
A quiet ibis wades in a pond and uses its long bill to find insects to eat.

R A beautiful rose grows on a bush. Watch out for the thorns.
A rabbit tries to hide by sitting very, very still. If you come too close, it will hop away fast.

S Long shadows of trees stretch across the snow-covered lawn.
A bright yellow sunflower can grow very tall.

T An old oak tree stretches out strong branches.
Tulips are cheerful spring flowers that grow from bulbs.

U Virginia creeper vines likes to climb up fences.
Lizards will hide under branches waiting to catch a tasty bug.

V Sometimes a shy violet will hide away in the lawn.

A vine will wrap, creep, and twirl around whatever it can climb.

W A pond full of water make a good home for a yellow waterlily. Plants need water to live.

A large ruffled white peony flower blooms in May. Peonies can also be pink and red.

X It's fun to explore a garden and see what you can find. What is in your garden?

A summer thunderstorm can be exciting, but it means get inside your house fast!

Y Bright yellow marigolds are an easy flower to grow in your garden.

A young groundhog is cute, but he likes to sneak under the fence and eat garden plants.

Z A zinnia is an annual that blooms in bright colors from summer until frost.

A busy bumblebee makes a happy buzzZZ as it collects pollen on a clematis flower.

About the Author

Jamie B. Banta is a teacher and loves encouraging new readers and writers as they explore their growing abilities. Her class cheers when it's time for their spelling test!

When not dreaming up stories, she enjoys taking photographs and gardening.

She lives in New Jersey with her husband and extremely spoiled cat Pookie.

JamieBeeDesigns.com/books

Facebook.com/JamieBanta

Twitter.com/JamieBeeDesigns

www.ingramcontent.com/pod-product-compliance
Lightning Source LLC
Chambersburg PA
CBHW050756110526
44588CB00002B/16